FOREIGN LANGUAGES AND CAREERS

Lucille J. Honig
and Richard I. Brod

Second Edition

The Modern Language Association of America
62 Fifth Avenue, New York, N.Y. 10011

102703

The original version of this pamphlet was prepared pursuant to a contract with the Office of Education, U.S. Department of Health, Education, and Welfare. Contractors undertaking such projects under government sponsorship are encouraged to express freely their judgment in professional and technical matters. Points of view or opinions do not, therefore, necessarily represent official Office of Education position or policy.

The revisions in this second edition are largely the work of Kristin Helmers, whose assistance is gratefully acknowledged.

Contents

INTRODUCTION

LANGUAGE AS AUXILIARY SKILL

Business and Commerce
Executive and Managerial — Technical and Engineering Positions — Banking and Financial Personnel — Secretarial and Clerical Staff

Civil Service
Local Government — Federal Government: Foreign Service — International Communication Agency — Other Agencies — Peace Corps, VISTA, Office of Economic Opportunity

Education
Research — Teaching — Administration — Schools Abroad — Teacher Exchanges — Federal Government — Company Schools Abroad

Law
Legal Aid — International Law — International Business

Library Science
Cataloging — Reference Libraries — Archives — Academic Libraries — Urban Libraries — Area Studies Specialists

Media
Journalism — Radio and Television — Film — Publishing

Science
Scientific Research — International Cooperation — Science and Industry

Service Occupations
Health Services — Social Work — Religious Occupations — Other Service Organizations

Social Sciences
Anthropology — Political Science — Sociology

Travel and Tourism
Hotels and Motels — Transportation

LANGUAGE AS PRIMARY SKILL

Foreign Language Teaching
Interpreting and Translating

SUMMARY

MATERIALS RELATING TO CAREERS USING LANGUAGES

USEFUL ADDRESSES

Introduction

A NEW YORK CITY taxi driver loses a fare because he doesn't know Spanish. — A corporate president waits in silence while an interpreter closes a deal with important Japanese investors. — A nurse in Maine can't diagnose a complaint because the patient is from Quebec and speaks only French. — An aspiring opera singer adores *Così fan tutte*, but can't understand, or pronounce, a word of it. — A government scientist learns about the latest breakthrough in solar energy a full year after it happened because the news was first published in Russian. All of these people could do their work better if they knew a foreign language, yet none of their jobs would seem to *require* a language. And what about journalists, television announcers, librarians, social workers, flight attendants, anthropologists, clergy, or chemists? According to the *Occupational Outlook Handbook* published by the U.S. Department of Labor, foreign languages are important for all these positions — a fact that is becoming more and more evident to readers of "help wanted" ads. A single edition of the *Los Angeles Times*, for example, included openings for a driving instructor, dental assistant, camera salesman, personnel manager, painter, carpenter, secretary, optician, carpet salesman, electronics teacher, factory foreman, and auto mechanic. *All* these jobs require a second language.

The connection between foreign languages and jobs may not be obvious to people who assume that foreign languages are used only by interpreters, translators, or foreign language teachers. But if one has another skill — almost any other marketable skill — *plus* a foreign language, one's chances of finding an interesting job are much often better than those of someone who has no language skills at all. Today's job market is difficult: employers can afford to be highly selective, and an extra skill often makes the difference. A good engineer who speaks German is more likely to be hired by a Swiss firm's American branch than an engineer with equivalent qualifications who speaks only English. A sales manager who knows Portuguese has a better chance of getting a highly paid assignment in Brazil than one who doesn't. The *Times* advertisement for

a Spanish-speaking driving instructor is another case in point. That driving school isn't going to settle for someone who speaks no Spanish or just a little Spanish. Only the applicant who really knows Spanish and is an experienced driving teacher as well has a good chance of getting the job.

Recently a major American auto manufacturer looked for public relations people who spoke German or French to work for its European plant and found only *five* in the entire country who had both the language skills and a good background in communications. In 1978, when the United States first established formal diplomatic relations with the People's Republic of China, there were embarrassingly few American journalists abroad who could speak Chinese. Indeed, between 1965 and 1978, Columbia University's Graduate Program in East Asian Journalism, the only U.S. program in existence that combines language study with professional journalistic training, had produced only fifteen or sixteen graduates who were fluent in Chinese or Japanese, and not all of these were working abroad. Of the thousands of federal government jobs overseas that require a foreign language, only about *half* are filled with people who know the languages well. Because of the international monetary situation, the number of foreign tourists visiting the United States has begun to equal or surpass the number of American tourists going abroad, yet many of America's hotels and motels still do not have bilingual or multilingual staff members in key guest-contact positions. Contrary to the assumption that jobs for language specialists are few in number and limited in scope, there are a number of jobs begging for people with language skills — but language skills as a *supplement* to other technical, business, or professional talents.

In a survey of American business, industry, and service organizations conducted by the Modern Language Association of America (MLA), nearly 70 percent of the respondents said they do employ, could employ or expect to employ people with foreign language skills.[1] For

---

[1] "Survey of Foreign Language Skills in Business and Service Organizations," *ADFL Bulletin* (Association of Departments of Foreign Languages), 5, No. 2 (November 1973), pp. 3-4. The research for this survey was conducted at the office of the Modern Language Association by Susan

some positions, knowledge of at least one foreign language is a specific requirement. For many others, it is an enormous help or a tool that is used regularly. For still others, it represents the kind of educational background and skills development that many employers want — whether they need specific languages or not. A substantial number of employers stated that, given two job candidates with equal abilities in their area of specialization, they would hire the one who knows a foreign language. This is true of employers all across the country and in American offices outside the country in areas as diverse as manufacturing, health care, government, banking, and social service.

Here are some of the comments made by employers in response to the survey:

> We need more executives with foreign language competence. They're hard to find. (Book publisher)

> One of the social workers here speaks fluent Spanish and she does a lot of work. The patients know that, so they come here. (Hospital nurse)

> As business becomes more multilingual in character, the demand for international banking services will increase, thereby creating needs for more personnel with foreign language skills. (Bank executive)

> We prefer someone with strong business experience who has language skill in addition. (Manufacturer)

> The need for foreign languages will increase on a professional level as worldwide activity in the foreign purchase of equipment, crude oil, and natural gas increases. (Utility company representative)

> A little skill is not enough. To be considered helpful, foreign language skill for an executive should be an all-around tool. . . . (Business executive)

> A candidate for a professional position is not considered unless he has a foreign language. (Library director)

Why have foreign languages become so important? Everyone agrees that the world is continually growing smaller. An airplane flight across the Atlantic took 17½ hours in 1947; today the SST can cover the distance between New York and Paris in less than one-quarter of

Hecker. Cheryl Dernorsek contributed to the refinement and organization of the material, and F. William D. Love assisted with the writing of the report.

that time. The number of passengers on trans-Atlantic flights has increased by one thousand percent. A telephone call to Sweden is almost as easy as a telephone call to the house next door. We can see European news on television live via satellite, and a French film, a Russian ballet, or a Japanese puppet show are often as close as the nearest theater. A dispute between two foreign countries is immediately felt in American political circles, while a major scientific discovery in any nation takes on worldwide significance almost at once.

Just as important as the internationalization of travel, the arts, media, politics, science, and technology is the economic interdependence of the world's nations. The United States, once intent on self-sufficiency, increasingly relies on foreign nations for vital natural resources, for monetary stability, and for a healthy balance of trade. We are dependent on foreign markets and on foreign suppliers more than ever before. International business connections exist all over the United States, not only in port cities, like New York or San Francisco, but wherever industry is located: the South, the Mississippi Valley, the Southwest, the Rocky Mountains, and Alaska. Nor are the effects of these connections felt exclusively among the growing number of big businesses that have offices overseas or deal in imports and exports. Even the corner grocer and the local garage mechanic deal with foreign products, and their involvement with them is likely to grow.

The number of countries involved with American business, as well as the extent of that involvement, is continually expanding. Japan is not only making considerable investment in American industry, but is also our chief competitor and trading partner and is expected to share one-quarter of the world export market with the United States by 1985. We have begun trade with China; the Arab nations are critical to the survival of our economy; Latin America and Africa are providing more and more opportunities for investment and trade. In short, America must prepare itself to deal extensively with foreign countries in commerce and industry. And in dealing with them we must realize that we cannot expect them to meet us solely on our own terms and in our own language. This is particularly true for business relations with developing nations whose growing national sensitivity has made the "Ugly American" and the "gringo" business executive more unwelcome than ever.

A California chamber of commerce executive, speaking from his own experience, sums up the need for languages in international business:

> Even in our Long Beach business community, where we have a major port and especially close ties with Japan, we have experienced a dramatic increase in correspondence and personal contact with citizens or spokesmen from other countries including the Soviet Union and Mainland China.
>
> An examination of my personal calendar for the month of October alone shows a dozen entries that involved appointments, meetings, or conferences of an international nature. A casual look at the content of major business publications that cross my desk turns up a myriad of titles dealing with international subjects. . . .
>
> If I could turn back the clock on my life, my approach to foreign languages would have been far less casual than it was, and I would now be in a position to be far more effective as a representative of my own community and country. . . . In this regard, I've tried to offset the deficiency with long hours of study at home on the language, history, and culture of Japan which has been my professional specialty for about twenty years.
>
> The world has become our main street, but the basic American insensitivity to other cultures prevails. It will continue to prevail as long as we continue to place the entire burden of language and cultural assimilation on our foreign friends. This was dangerous enough when the world was much larger and we were separated by great oceans. In recent years, it has led to monstrous errors and miscalculations in foreign policy, trade relations, and decision making within business and industry. *The inability of the average American to communicate in the most elementary way in a second language continues to breed resentment in the minds of our friends in other countries.* Like it or not, we must accept the fact that America does not stand alone as an economic superpower. There are now four or five countries in that category and the United States will have to work hard just to stay in the ball game. Today, and in tomorrow's world, the young man or woman of America who is fluent in a second language has a very bright future indeed.[2]

But it is not only in dealing with other countries that the need for foreign language skills arises. In recent years, as America began feel-ing a more urgent need for languages in international politics and commerce certain ethnic groups in the United States also reached a state of self-awareness in which total assimilation into the "melting pot" was no longer a pressing goal. Instead, the preservation of their original cultural identities—traditions, lifestyles, and languages—became a major concern. The reality and the value of a diverse and multilingual society have become accepted as facts of American life. Spanish, for example, is no longer a foreign language, but truly a second language in many parts of the country. Courses such as Commercial Spanish, and Spanish for Medical Personnel are now routine offerings at many community colleges, urban colleges, and nonacademic institutions. In addition, the ethnic communities of the United States are of steadily growing commercial importance, and a properly keyed sales talk in Spanish may be as vital to the success of a product in New York or Houston as it is in Buenos Aires or Madrid. Indeed, in any area of the country where there are large minority communities—and this means almost every big city and many towns and rural areas as well—knowledge of a foreign language can be useful for *any* job. One language school in the West, for instance, has enrolled doctors, business executives, lawyers, airline pilots, actors, police officers, nurses, teachers, flight attendants, social workers, and real estate agents.

The purpose of this report is to explain why so many different types of people in so many different parts of the country need languages in their work and why students planning their education in preparation for certain careers should be aware of these needs. The focus is mainly on language as an auxiliary skill, on the careers in which languages are most likely to be needed, and on the ways in which foreign language skills can help in individual jobs. Also discussed are careers for language specialists—foreign language teaching, translating, and interpreting.

[2] Ernest LaBelle, "The World Is Your Main Street," *Forum* (Modern and Classical Language Association of Southern California), 12, No. 2 (January 1974), pp. 4-5.

LANGUAGE AS AUXILIARY SKILL

Business and Commerce

Most big business in America today is truly international in scope. Some 3,800 United States firms have branches or representatives abroad, resulting in an annual overseas production estimated at $500 billion; over 2,300 foreign businesses have interests in the United States. In addition, the United States ranks as the world's largest trading nation, with exports totaling $121 billion in 1977 (excluding military aid) and imports in the same year exceeding $147 billion.

What is the language of international business? Undoubtedly, English is the most widely used language. Yet there are many reasons why it cannot be safely assumed that English is sufficient for all purposes in the complex world of business. For example, representatives of an American firm abroad often need to deal directly—without an intermediary or interpreter—with foreign personnel, local government agencies, clients, and competitors. Employees in American branches of foreign firms continually need to refer to the home office for instructions, policy decisions, and product information. Furthermore, selling American products, especially consumer goods, abroad often requires an intimate knowledge of the culture of the foreign nation, the kind of knowledge that is based upon close acquaintance with the history, customs, media, language, and social institutions of the foreign country. In short, a second language can be a key to success, and a U.S. business representative who lacks knowledge of that language may unexpectedly become dependent upon interpreters to get business done—a dependence that may prove both disadvantageous and costly to the U.S. firm.

A large number of businesses surveyed by the MLA indicated that foreign languages are used in their offices both in the United States and abroad by employees at all levels—executive, managerial, technical, and secretarial. For some, language skill is a requirement; for others, it is useful on numerous occasions; for still others, it is an educational asset that may contribute to the general usefulness of the employee. Many companies state that they will give language training to their employees when the need arises; others who might be willing to provide it often find the costs prohibitive. Lacking American personnel with language competence, firms are often compelled to hire and train foreign nationals for their overseas positions. A study conducted in Minnesota revealed that the larger businesses tend to follow this practice, while smaller American firms prefer to "export" their American employees.

Executive and Managerial Positions

As they expand their business efforts overseas, American firms are increasingly on the lookout for executives and managerial staff who know a second language, for both their home and overseas offices. In the Minnesota study, for example, several companies responded that *all* of their management staff spoke, and used, a foreign language. The MLA survey showed that language skills sometimes mean better chances for promotion, higher salaries, and attractive assignments overseas. Even when languages are not required, many companies indicated that, when hiring new management personnel, they give preference to candidates with foreign language skills, provided other business experience and abilities are equal. Here are just a few of the responses received from corporations during the survey:

> A year and a half ago we reorganized on a world-wide products line basis and have thus become a truly multinational corporation. One result of this is that there is a growing interest on the part of executives to develop proficiency in a second language. For the future I am convinced increasing attention will be paid to foreign language skills. . . .

> Our experience in Latin America has suggested strongly the application of our current policy which is to hire only executives with Spanish or Portuguese language proficiency.

> Employees with a knowledge of foreign languages definitely have an advantage for executive positions overseas, both in being selected and in future promotion.

> With increasing involvement by [our company] in Europe, Central and South America, and the Far East, we will require broad-minded executives who can acquire a new language in order to quickly assimilate customs, business conditions, and trade requirements around the world. The

"Ugly American" should be passé in business if the U.S. is to compete in world trade. We will emphasize the need for foreign language ability by executives as we acquire new talent.

The type of company that needs management staff with foreign language skills, the languages needed, and the technical or business experience required vary widely, covering a wide spectrum of the business world from the oil and aerospace industries to manufacturers of metal products, jewelry, textiles, and pharmaceutical supplies, to mention only a few. For example, one issue of the *New York Times* listed job openings for production managers, marketing managers, and general managers for both domestic and overseas assignments with packaged food companies and cosmetics manufacturers. The positions offered salaries ranging from $14,000 to $50,000 and required fluent language ability—for one position, fluency in French, German, *and* Spanish; for another, French and German; and for a third, French, German, or Italian. Another opening for an international marketing production manager for a pharmaceutical company required Spanish or Portuguese. A position as assistant to the vice-president of export operations demanded fluent Spanish, while an advertising manager, with experience in media, sales, promotion, and budgeting, needed both an unspecified second language and a degree in business administration. Fluent Spanish was a requirement for a $25,000-a-year position as an international marketing coordinator with a research background and experience in pharmaceutical or health care products to coordinate market demands between Latin America and the United States. And the *Washington Post* carried an advertisement for an import-export manager who spoke English, Korean, and Japanese.

Perhaps even more convincing than company statements and job offerings are comments made by executives themselves. Many who frequently come into contact with foreign business executives or who have direct involvements abroad have repeatedly stated that knowledge of a foreign language is an enormous advantage and that lack of language skills is a real handicap. For example, the vice-president of one corporation stated:

I, as the Director of this Company, am convinced that foreign language skills are an absolute necessity from a commercial point of view. I am a native American, for example, speaking practically fluent French, and moderate Spanish. I am, however, severely limited by my lack of good conversational ability in Spanish and this factor must be compensated for by other employees in my company with a better (or perfect) knowledge of Spanish, but with lesser managerial and administrative abilities. There is no question in my mind that the person with a command of more than English will succeed—all other factors being equal—over one who speaks English only.

The president of a southern export business also speaks from personal experience in discussing the importance of language skills in international business:

With regard to the conduct of business, there is most definitely a frustration involved in not being able to understand what other parties are saying during negotiations, even where common language is being used for negotiations proper. . . . The knowledge of even a few words of the opposite side's language in business contacts warms up the atmosphere.

There is no question that even though our company is essentially American in feeling, method of operations, and personnel, we have been unusually successful in Latin America where other, larger U.S. companies have either failed or fallen short. There is no doubt in my mind that a major factor has been the multilingual ability of the staff and personnel which makes Latin American business people classify our company as non-gringo.

I have tried to establish Latin American business ties since 1959. I finally decided to concentrate on learning Spanish around 1965, and after I became proficient in 1967, my business with Spanish-speaking countries soared from nothing to over twenty million dollars yearly.

. . . Visiting foreign business [executives] never fail to be pleasantly surprised when they visit our offices and find personnel able to converse with them in their language. Often they are swept off their feet. . . .

Even though English *is* the international business language, those [persons] for whom it is not their native tongue seem to put an extra effort and enthusiasm into conducting or concluding business where the conversation is in their native language or in a language foreign to both parties.

... It is inconceivable that ... American [business executives], with over one hundred million dollars invested outside the United States, often must put [their] faith in the native bilingual chauffeur or taxi driver in order to find [their] way to [their] newly built plant or newly organized offices.[3]

Technical and Engineering Positions

Most likely to need technical and engineering staff with language proficiency are companies with overseas plants, those that manufacture machinery that is used overseas, American subsidiaries of European-based companies, and manufacturers who use European-made components in their American operations. One company in South Carolina, for example, produces textile machinery using both European- and American-made parts:

> In order to successfully accomplish this joining of components produced in different countries, built under systems of different measurements and different specifications, we need engineering and technical personnel capable of communicating in various languages. All the drawings, all the descriptions, all the technical material sent to us by our foreign suppliers are, as a rule, in a foreign language and must be translated by us for our own use, as well as for the convenience of our customers.[4]

Another firm notes that it employs a few people in the technical field who translate technical papers from German into English. Still another stated that its most specific need at the time was for laboratory technicians with a reading knowledge of German who could make use of German-language research material to further their own work. And the Twin Cities study revealed that in the Minneapolis-St. Paul area there is a demand for technicians, draftsmen, and people trained in repair work—all with foreign language skills—to service systems and machinery produced in that area to be sold and installed abroad.

One American branch of a German company notes that while its employees are not hired for their language skills, those who possess them have a definite asset:

> In our company the German language is of advantage and would certainly contribute to chances of employment, all other aspects being

equal. This refers primarily to the Engineering and Process Application areas where we are still occasionally corresponding in German with our partners to avoid any misunderstanding in technical translations from Germany. We are also doing a considerable amount of conversion of German drawings to the American system and this, of course, could be simplified if someone could read a German drawing.

Another firm that is involved in overseas business states that it could use bilingual and multilingual employees in the technical field both in the United States and abroad and implies that such personnel are not readily available:

> For a company such as ours, someone with foreign language and the ability to go to the countries concerned and discuss technical matters with the people in their own language would certainly be a tremendous advantage to us, even more so would be the ability to communicate with the engineers sent here from foreign countries to install machinery in this country. We have quite a few instances where the ability to speak French, Italian, and German would have been valuable.

A large chemical company with extensive involvement abroad pointed out that it seldom hires an employee on the basis of his language skill alone; like many other large American companies, most of its employees overseas are natives of the foreign countries. However, U.S. employees with second language skills are still considered a definite asset to the company:

> Foreign language skills of regular staff members are utilized even though they were not hired for this purpose. Employee data, readily available from the computer, can provide the necessary match between the particular language and technical background required for a particular assignment. As an example, a former U.S. employee with an engineering background is currently assigned to one of our European locations as a technical representative because he happens to be fluent in the Russian language.

[3] André Crispin, "Foreign Languages beyond the Campus," *ADFL Bulletin*, 5, No. 3 (March 1974), pp. 49-50.

[4] Quoted by Edwin Arnold, "The Importance of Foreign Languages to Foreign Industry in South Carolina," unpublished survey, 1972. American Association of Teachers of German, South Carolina Chapter.

Finally, some companies do try to hire American technicians with specific language skills for overseas work, as did the company that put this ad in the *Los Angeles Times.*

> Overseas Assignment. We have immediate openings for Senior Planning and Scheduling Engineers, Senior Cost Engineers, and Senior Estimators for an Assignment in Peru. Familiarity with CPM, cost engineering, planning and scheduling, and estimating techniques is essential. A minimum of 5 years experience in engineering and construction industry, preferably in mining and metals. An engineering degree is preferred. *Working knowledge of Spanish is desirable.*

Banking and Financial Personnel

With the expansion of international business operations, the expansion of international banking and finance activities naturally follows, accompanied by an increasing need for foreign language as an adjunct skill in the financial world. In one *New York Times* Sunday classified section, for example, twenty-five percent of the ads for nonsecretarial bilingual employees were in the financial area. These included:

> —An associate vice-president with knowledge of French and Arabic for a Middle Eastern office of a New York bank
> —Two Spanish-speaking auditors
> —A Spanish-speaking accountant
> —Two banking correspondents with "knowledge of bank operations, letters of credit, or paying and receiving," plus fluency in French, German, or Italian, to work with customer accounts
> —An Arabic-speaking territorial bank officer
> —A bank credit analyst with fluent French
> —A Spanish-speaking commercial lending officer to serve as a bank's area representative in South America
> —A bank credit analyst with fluency in Spanish and an accounting background to interpret corporate and foreign bank credit data
> —A multilingual international banking administrative assistant
> —An international marketing and financial assistant with a technical degree and knowledge of at least one foreign language

Banks surveyed by the MLA reported that among their bilingual and multilingual personnel were overseas representatives and international banking officers, as well as translators, domestic banking officers, and clerks for some areas in the United States. Some banks hire Spanish-speaking personnel for their branches in predominantly Spanish-speaking neighborhoods, for example, while others need bilingual employees to satisfy both international business and local community needs, as in the case of this accounts clerk for a Japanese bank in California:

> As new accounts clerk for the Mitsubishi Bank of California, I must be able to communicate with every customer of the Bank from those representing large Japanese corporations to those holding only small individual accounts. I have appeared in Japanese language television commercials for the Bank. Many Japanese customers are surprised and very pleased by a non-Japanese speaking to them in their native tongue. I enjoy dealing with the public, and the Japanese language aspect of my job often adds a stimulating challenge rewarded by a personal satisfaction in being able to assist both Japanese and American customers, and a professional satisfaction in assisting the development of a new bank.[5]

One executive of a large New York bank notes that any of his bank's employees interested in an international career and overseas assignments should have a command of at least two foreign languages, one of which should be French or Spanish. Another major bank with operations abroad needs employees with an aptitude for financial analysis *and* knowledge of foreign countries, cultures, and languages for its international division assignments in New York and in about fifteen locations abroad. This bank prefers to hire people for its overseas positions who have lived or studied abroad or have completed area studies programs at college, either at the undergraduate or graduate level. And its representative sums up the views of many banks, as well as other business interests, when he says, "Dealing with a customer in his own language is in some instances a necessity and in every circumstance an advantage."

Secretarial and Clerical Staff

One of the largest markets for bilingual personnel is in the secretarial and clerical area. In

[5] Quoted in "Foreign Languages and Your Career," *Forum* (MCLASC), 12, No. 2 (January 1974), p. 8.

many cases executives and managerial staff do not have language skills themselves and must hire assistants who do have them. Corporations with branches or activities overseas, import-export firms, banks, and international brokerage firms are the most frequent employers of bilingual secretaries in the business sector. Bilingual medical secretaries and secretarial staff for service and cultural organizations, small businesses, and local and government agencies are also frequently in demand in communities where there are sizeable concentrations of minority groups.

Most bilingual secretarial jobs require skills in typing and either shorthand or dictaphone transcription. Those that require shorthand usually require it in the foreign language as well as in English. Other responsibilities often include research, correspondence, bookkeeping, switchboard or telephone service, and translating. Fluency in the foreign language is usually a must, particularly for such duties as reading, writing, or typing business correspondence in a foreign language, translating technical papers, or arranging meetings with foreign executives. A bilingual secretary should also be familiar with the industry involved and fluent in its specialized vocabulary, in both English and the foreign language, including technical terminology in such areas as banking, import-export, or engineering.

In one Sunday edition of the *New York Times*, 54 out of 102 job listings for bilingual personnel were for secretaries, typists, and receptionists. French, Spanish, and German were the languages most frequently called for, while Italian, Portuguese, Japanese, and Arabic were required for a few positions. In addition, several openings required skills in two languages other than English, such as Spanish and Portuguese, German and French, or German and Spanish. A majority of the ads offered positions in the business and marketing world. For example, several import-export firms dealing in such commodities as tires, perfumes, packaged foods, and jewelry needed bilingual secretaries for their trade or marketing divisions. There were also jobs with an architectural consulting firm, a foreign consulate, a travel agency, a music publisher, and an art gallery. Almost all the positions offered salaries higher than the average salary for secretaries with English language skills only.

The need for foreign languages in secretarial work is not limited to any one region of the country. Many firms in southern states such as South Carolina and Georgia indicate that they employ secretaries with skills in German, French, and Spanish. In the West, there is a demand for Spanish-speaking secretarial staff in all areas of business and in the service fields and a growing need for secretaries with a thorough knowledge of Japanese. And in a survey of businesses in the Minneapolis-St. Paul area, many personnel directors indicated that skills in foreign languages combined with typing, shorthand, and accounting vocabulary would be a "definite asset" and that there was also some need for secretarial staff with a knowledge of drafting vocabulary in Spanish, German, and Japanese. The Minnesota state employment agency reported that there were, at the time of the survey, twelve positions for bilingual secretaries and documentation personnel available, but that there were no qualified people to fill them.

There are also some opportunities for American secretaries to work abroad in agencies of the federal government or in foreign offices of American corporations. In almost every case in which American secretaries are assigned overseas, they start out in the firm's American offices, as in the following "success story," published in the newsletter of a Colorado teachers' association:

> Barbara M—, a 1971 graduate of Pueblo Senior High School, because of her outstanding ability in both business and French, is now working for the Bank of America in Paris, France. . . . Immediately after graduating she got a job in San Francisco with Bank Americard. Her employer had the opportunity to transfer to Paris and . . . because of her knowledge of the French language, she was able to transfer with him.[6]

In this instance, the extra dimension of language skill enabled the secretary to enhance her usefulness to future employers by adding foreign work experience to her other qualifications.

[6] Quoted in *Peals* (Colorado Congress of Foreign Language Teachers), 14, No. 1 (September 1973), p. 2.

Civil Service

Civil servants carry out the work of local, state, and federal government. Although one out of every six Americans can be classified as a civil servant, the range of their occupations is so diverse that it includes jobs unique to government as well as nearly every kind of job found in the private sector. A civil servant could be an administrator, postal worker, police officer, doctor, judge, secretary, counselor, plumber, scientist, teacher, draftsman, or just about any other kind of employee.

At all levels of government, an employee is most likely to use language skills as a supplement to other skills and knowledge and must generally pass a competitive examination testing that knowledge in order to qualify for a civil service position. On the local level, the degree to which foreign languages are used depends largely on the ethnic make-up of the community. In any area where there are sizeable concentrations of immigrant or minority groups, there are some positions where languages are required and others where they would be a definite advantage. In New York City, for example, police officers are not required to know a second language, but more than 500 of them are enrolled each semester in Spanish courses offered by the City University of New York because they find it difficult to perform their duties without a knowledge of Spanish.

Besides being the largest employer in the United States, with a work force of two and one-half million people, the federal government is the largest employer of individuals with foreign language skills, both in the United States and abroad. Recognizing the importance of language proficiency in overseas service, it has established a category of language-essential positions in the Department of State, the Agency for International Development, the International Communication Agency (formerly the U.S. Information Agency), and various other branches of government. A recent federal report, however, shows that only about *one-half* of these positions are satisfactorily filled. In fact, the combination of language skills with political, diplomatic, or administrative training is so rare that in the Department of State, only 57 percent of the positions for which languages are essential are adequately filled. And during the war in Southeast Asia, only 15 percent of the 144 civilian positions requiring the Thai language were filled by employees with a working knowledge of that language. The recognition of a need for improvement in these areas signals an increase in opportunities for government employees with strong language backgrounds.

Of the nearly 15,000 persons employed by the Department of State, more than 10,000 serve abroad. The department's foreign service officers may be political specialists who maintain close contact with foreign officials, or they may specialize in economic and commercial work, promoting American trade, helping American businesses abroad, or reporting to Washington on local business conditions, monetary fluctuations, and trade patterns. There are also consular positions such as visa or passport and citizenship officers, and a variety of administrative functions exists. All of these positions involve extensive contact with foreign citizens.

Foreign service officers are selected on the basis of examinations that test their general knowledge and aptitude for international relations. Many have college training in subjects such as economics, languages, political science, and area studies. All receive special training after entering the Department of State. And although only 1,217 department positions overseas are considered language-essential, languages are still extremely important for every foreign service officer, not just in terms of job performance, but also in terms of promotion and salary, as stated in a Department of State booklet, *Foreign Service Officer:*

> Knowledge of a foreign language is not a requirement for appointment to the Foreign Service. After appointment, however, officers are expected to acquire an acceptable level of proficiency in at least one foreign language, and junior officers are limited to no more than one promotion until they do so. New officers are given language tests after they enter on duty. Those who pass a speaking and reading test in one of 30 or more foreign languages will end their language probation and may in some instances become eligible to receive a higher salary in their officer class.[7]

[7]U.S. Dept. of State, *Foreign Service Officer*, 1978, p. 9.

The International Communication Agency also employs foreign service officers with a wide variety of backgrounds in such areas as media, education, and business for its cultural and information programs around the world. In addition, the agency employs secretaries, librarians, and, on a temporary basis, many types of professionals such as lawyers, teachers, and agricultural specialists. It also sponsors the Voice of America radio broadcasting office, which employs writers, editors, and announcers for broadcasts in numerous languages. These jobs require native fluency in the language and, for announcers, nearly perfect pronunciation.

Several other government departments and agencies require language skills for specific positions. Speakers of Slavic, Middle Eastern, and Far Eastern languages are employed by the Department of Defense as translators, research assistants, and communications experts within the National Security Agency. The Federal Bureau of Investigation employs linguists and also makes use of the language skills of its special agents. The Agency for International Development employs nearly 3,000 people to work overseas. Border patrol officials for the Immigration and Naturalization Service must speak Spanish, and, like customs officials, they have occasion to use many other languages. The Drug Enforcement Administration employs Americans who are fluent in the languages of the countries where they are stationed. All branches of the armed services have certain language-essential positions. And some positions in the Department of Treasury's Foreign Claims Settlement Commission require foreign languge skills as a supplement to legal training.

Finally, some service-oriented government organizations frequently demand foreign language skills. The Peace Corps employs 6,500 volunteers, all of whom must be trained in the language of the country to which they are assigned. VISTA, the "domestic Peace Corps," needs some volunteers who know Spanish, French, or Indian languages. And the Office of Economic Opportunity requires language skills for employees in its community action programs such as Head Start and its legal services, health centers, and programs for migrant workers and Indians.

Education

Education is one of the largest "industries" in the United States, involving about 60 million students and employing nearly three million teachers and administrators. There are three major aspects of education: research, administration, and teaching. Knowledge of a foreign language can be important in all three areas.

The importance of foreign language proficiency to persons doing advanced research is demonstrated by the fact that most master's degree programs and virtually all doctoral programs require some foreign language study. Most research and graduate study are international in their coverage, and a great deal of original research material, as well as reports of prior research, is available only in languages other than English. Serious researchers need at least a functional reading knowledge of the languages relevant to their work. In some fields, such as anthropology, sociology, religion, urbanology, political science, or comparative and foreign literatures, the need is self-evident. In others, the need for a foreign language is less obvious, but no less real. In meteorology, physics, geology, mathematics, chemistry, and the biological sciences, for example, up to 30 percent of published research is in Russian, and nearly 15 percent is in French or German. Translation agencies exist, but they are frequently slow, do not translate all the material available, and usually do only abstracts of articles. Obviously researchers who can make use of material in the foreign language will be able to do much more with their subjects and will be in a better position than colleagues who know only English.

In the fields of academic administration and teaching, foreign languages are likely to be of direct importance if one comes in contact with non-English-speaking students or community and parents' groups. Traditionally it has not been necessary for teachers and administrators to learn the languages of parents and students; school was the institution that socialized students, pulling them away from their ethnic cultures and into the English-speaking mainstream. Increasingly, however, schools are being asked to help preserve ethnic cultures in America—at least the language of a particular culture. In these situations, a knowledge of foreign languages will help teachers and administrators to be more effective.

Opportunities for teachers with foreign language skills also exist in schools abroad, where they might often teach English, American civilization, or other subjects for which there might be a shortage of qualified local teachers. Generally such teachers are required to have at least a college minor in the field they will teach as well as a background in the foreign and American cultures and a working knowledge of the foreign language. Information about such teaching jobs may be obtained from the Institute for International Education (see appendix).

Under the provisions of the Fulbright-Hays Act, an elementary or secondary school teacher can participate in a direct exchange of positions with a teacher from abroad or may simply be placed in a foreign school. To be eligible for the exchange program, a teacher must have three years of full-time teaching experience and a college degree; there are 135 openings each year. Inquiries can be addressed to the Teacher Exchange Section of the U.S. Office of Education (see appendix).

The Departments of Education in the territories and possessions of the United States also hire American teachers with foreign language skills for their schools. Information concerning such positions can be obtained by writing to the Director of Education in American Samoa, Canal Zone, Guam, Mariana Islands, Puerto Rico, and Virgin Islands.

There are also teaching opportunities within several branches of the federal government. The army, navy, and air force operate schools abroad, known as Overseas Dependents Schools, for the children of their personnel located in foreign countries. Teachers of foreign languages are also hired by the Department of Defense for the army, navy, and air force academies in the United States. The International Communication Agency employs teachers in its Bi-national Centers abroad; usually these teachers are assigned to teach English or American Studies. The Agency for International Development, a separate agency of the Department of State, sends education specialists abroad, but they are more likely to work as advisors or administrators than as classroom teachers.

Finally, a number of American corporations with overseas offices have set up schools abroad for the children of their employees. Among these corporations are Firestone, Gulf Oil, Exxon, and the United Fruit Company.

Law

Knowledge of a foreign language can be a direct, practical asset to the lawyer who works frequently with members of ethnic minority and immigrant groups, does legal aid work, or specializes in international law, maritime law, or international business. In these fields, lawyers who lack language skills may find themselves dependent upon the services of translators and other intermediaries, an arrangement that is time-consuming, awkward for both lawyer and client, and in many cases expensive.

Lawyers serving corporations with overseas branches or with extensive foreign trade involvements also need skills in a foreign language if they are involved in obtaining contracts abroad, negotiating trade agreements with foreign executives, settling disputes or breaches of international contracts, counseling in matters of foreign tariff laws, or communicating with foreign personnel in American subsidiaries overseas. A classified advertisement in the *New York Times*, for instance, called for an international corporate attorney who "must be able to communicate effectively with both domestic and foreign clientele" and speak either French or German or both. And an American affiliate office of a German-based corporation considers it important to have "American lawyers who know enough German to represent the patent interests of the company in American courts." There are, in addition, some opportunities for lawyers with language skills to work abroad, on temporary or permanent assignments, for offices of American corporations or federal agencies.

A survey of law school admissions policies shows that most law schools are concerned more with the broad preparation of applicants than with the specific courses and majors they have had in college. They not only accept, but often prefer, law students with a liberal arts education rather than a narrow, strictly pre-law background.

[Professional law schools] are becoming increasingly interested in the applicant who has used his undergraduate education to explore various academic areas in an effort to gain a broad exposure to the humanities, a deeper insight into human behavior, and a mind that is trained to think critically and logically, to interpret rapidly and accurately, and to articulate its observations and conclusions with clarity and precision.[8]

The law board examinations required of law school applicants are designed primarily to test a student's analytical ability, reading comprehension, reasoning, general knowledge (including literature), and precision in the use of English. As an enhancement of students' ability to use the English language with skill, as well as a direct contribution to their knowledge of literature and the humanities, a major or minor in foreign languages can be excellent preparation for law school.

Library Science

Most graduate programs offering a master's degree in library science require that a student have a reading knowledge of at least one foreign language. This is no accident or arbitrary policy: almost all libraries—public, private, and academic—handle books, reference works, and periodicals in a number of different languages in a variety of fields.

To order and catalog a new book in a foreign language, a librarian must know enough of the language to have a general idea of what the book is about. Reference librarians should know at least one foreign language, and preferably more than one, in order to have access to as wide a range of reference materials as possible. The archives of some libraries offer opportunities for research and documentation specialists with language skills. Large college libraries frequently require librarians with a strong language background to work in their foreign-language literature collections. Many libraries in large cities have developed general reading and information sections for specific minority groups. In addition, some urban libraries are offering special programs—storytelling sessions, for instance—for Spanish-speaking residents, and need Spanish-speaking personnel to work in community service positions with both adults and children. And some

U.S. government agencies abroad employ librarians with a knowledge of local languages to work for their English language libraries around the world. The International Communication Agency, for example, has some 200 libraries in more than 80 countries.

Not all libraries specifically require prospective employees to know a second language, but nearly all benefit from those who do. One library reported that it considers language skills useful in about 75 percent of its positions at all levels. And the chances of employment for librarians with language specialties seem to be on the rise. In academic libraries in particular, the increase of African and Asian studies programs, as well as other area studies, and the acquisitioning of related original language materials have created a growing need for librarians with skills in the less commonly taught languages such as Chinese, Japanese, and Arabic. One college library also noted that more scientific, literary, economic, and philosophical works are now coming into the academic library in their original languages. Recognizing a similar trend elsewhere, nearly two-thirds of the libraries contacted in the MLA survey foresaw a growth in the number of foreign language materials they would purchase and a substantial growth in the need for language skills in years to come.

Media

Journalism

In journalism, as in other fields, foreign language skills are not the only key to employment, but they are an important asset. Most of the newspapers surveyed by the MLA said that there is some need for foreign languages in their profession and that language skills possessed by their employees are generally used to varying degrees. One newspaper in Florida, for instance, listed several uses for Spanish:

It is useful for our advertising salespeople to know Spanish in dealing with Spanish-speaking advertisers in our pages. . . . As to our Editorial Department, there is an occasional requirement to interview or get a story from a Spanish-speaking individual, [and] many of our editorial staffers

[8] Linwood E. Orange, *English: The Pre-Professional Major*, 3rd ed. (New York: Modern Language Association, 1979), p. 5.

16

have a proficiency in Spanish. Our Circulation Department might also have occasion to converse with someone who is Spanish-speaking.

A newspaper in Delaware notes that speaking and understanding Spanish can be "useful for a reporter with a number of assignments in Spanish-speaking neighborhoods." The editor of a daily paper in Louisiana reports that foreign language skills are necessary for a small number of his news staff and that several reporters speak and read French or Spanish. He also comments on the opportunity to use foreign languages in reporting international news:

> I am just back from [a] mission to Austria, Russia, Iran, and Poland with [the] President. One of our columnists is on a three month swing through Europe. Another of our writers returned within the past several weeks from a tour of observation in North and South America.

A midwest publisher cites two specific situations in which the command of one or more foreign languages is a practical asset to a journalist working for his two newspapers: first, interviewing foreign visitors, and second, translating an interesting, quotable item that appears in a foreign newspaper or magazine. Believing that a newspaper person should have a well-rounded education, this publisher regards the knowledge of a second language as a "necessary element in the culture of a prospective journalist." Another publisher agreed that skill in a foreign language "is one of those things which strongly suggests the kind of person who is the best kind of [journalist]."

For foreign correspondents working abroad for such organizations as the Associated Press or United Press International, or for large newspapers, weekly news magazines, or major television networks, there is a real need for fluency in foreign languages. But foreign correspondents are selected primarily on the basis of their skills as journalists; in the past, their language skills have often been inadequate or nonexistent. In the whole Middle East at the time of heightened Arab-Israeli conflicts, only *one* professional journalist spoke fluent Arabic and only a few spoke Hebrew. Certainly the speed at which news is transmitted, as well as the reporter's depth of understanding and ability to judge the authenticity of information,

could be improved if an intervening interpreter were left out.

Speaking from broad personal experience as a foreign correspondent, Loyal Gould, Chairman of the Department of Journalism at Wichita State University, says, "American journalism is in desperate need of journalists who have an understanding and perhaps even a sympathy for foreign nations and people."[9] He notes that there are only about 300 American correspondents abroad "at a time when the larger American news organizations would like to double if not triple their foreign news staffs" and at a time when events around the world bear increasing relevance to the people of the United States. He calls attention to a master's degree program in journalism at Ohio State University in which students are required to be fluent in a foreign language and, in addition, to spend a six-month internship in the part of the world where they want to be correspondents.

> The success of that program is attested by the fact that my former students are now scattered throughout the world in East and West Europe, Africa, the Middle East, Latin America, and Asia. . . . American journalism was eager for these young people because they had something to offer that was traditionally lacking among newspaper people.[10]

Among foreign correspondents it appears that there *is* a demand—and an increasing one —not only for top-rate reporting skills, but also for fluency in a foreign language and comprehensive understanding of the country or region of specialization.

Radio and Television

These media employ writers, directors, and editors, as well as executives, administrators, technicians, announcers, and performers. Many local stations, both private and public, are increasing the number of programs geared toward ethnic groups, and, as any *Sesame Street* viewer knows, Spanish is being used more and more often on educational television. The MLA survey found stations across the country

[9] Loyal Gould, "Languages in Communication: Expanded Opportunities for Language Majors in Business and Industry," *ADFL Bulletin*, 4, No. 3 (March 1973), p. 34.

[10] Gould, p. 35.

—in such states as Michigan, Maine, Rhode Island, California, New York, Mississippi, Virginia, and Washington—that were producing or planning to produce special programs for minority groups, and, in some cases, language education programs.

One television station in the West, for example, reported a need for Spanish staff members:

> We have a significant number of Spanish-speaking Americans living in the area served by this television station. Program producers, on-the-air talent, writers—whether staff or contractual—could serve as more superior communicators if they were bilingual in Spanish and English.

A New England station anticipates a need for language skills for its executives, both for services to minority groups in the community and for international television activities involving the exchange of programs and joint productions with networks abroad. In the Midwest, a station executive discussed the uses of knowledge of a second language and culture:

> In management, [we] consider [foreign language knowledge] a bonus. . . . In specialized areas of programming it is a necessity—but it is equally important in our case that the individual be knowledgeable of cultural and social aspects of the audience in question and that he or she be respected by that group.

In one Maine community with a large French-speaking population, special television programs in French are being planned even though the French-speaking residents also speak English; a representative of the station notes that having some bilingual staff and using French in programming add an extra dimension to the station's public relations, thus increasing its popularity and success.

Finally, in any part of the country, radio and television announcers must be able to pronounce foreign words and names correctly, whether reporting an international sports event, introducing a German opera, or conducting an interview with a political leader from abroad. This is particularly important for news reporters. At a time when events and people around the world are continually in the news, familiarity with several languages is indispensable to the news announcer who wants to be accurate.

Film

Not every aspiring performer can plan on working under the direction of Ingmar Bergman or co-starring with Catherine Deneuve. Yet skills in a second language can, in some instances, help those involved with film production, performance, and technical work, as well as the business and administrative side of the film industry in all kinds of productions, from the Hollywood extravaganza to the educational filmstrip.

People interested in film as an art—and as a career—expand their knowledge of the field when they can understand film classics in their original language, since dubbing and subtitles rarely can provide a complete translation or capture the significance of intonation and inflection. Of course, writing subtitles and dubbing films are themselves highly specialized jobs, requiring thorough knowledge of the foreign language involved, its slang and idiomatic expressions, as well as a background in cinematic techniques.

Film production is one of the most international of the arts and one in which technical skill and artistic talent transcend all national boundaries. It is not uncommon for foreign and American film crew members to cooperate on a single film. And, since authenticity of setting is crucial to visual effects, American film crews frequently do their filming abroad. Furthermore, there are films that deal specifically with other cultures and countries. These might include anything from a documentary on the problems of Mexican-American farm workers to a travel film about Rome or an educational film that teaches Russian. In instances such as these, performers, executives, writers, and technicians may need a foreign language in order to understand their topic, to communicate with the people being filmed, to communicate with one another on international crews, to prepare scripts, or simply to get along in the foreign country where they are working.

Distribution of American films abroad and importation of foreign films to the United States also provide opportunities for people with foreign language skills. One film company surveyed by the MLA replied that it had recently contracted for foreign film distribution, and that if this international aspect of its business increased as anticipated, it would need executives and clerical staff with foreign language skills. A company that produces documentary films noted several uses for foreign languages:

> In documentary film making, persons with foreign language skill have always been favored for work abroad and . . . for foreign producers working in the United States. Now we [also] expect an increase in production and exchange of educational films between countries.

Publishing

Foreign language skills are useful for editors, editorial assistants, executives, proofreaders, or secretaries in many publishing houses, particularly those that market their books abroad, deal extensively in translations, or specialize in educational materials. Language skills are needed in communicating with foreign publishers, distributors, and authors, in reviewing foreign language manuscripts for possible publication, and in editing and proofreading books published in their original language or in translation, foreign language textbooks, and English language books that include many foreign words.

One large book publisher requires foreign languages for its international salespeople as well as its copy editors, permissions correspondents, and editors of foreign language textbooks. Another publisher notes that in addition to hiring free-lance translators, the firm employs a multilingual translation editor who reviews announcements of forthcoming books, evaluates new books and journals published in other languages with a view toward possible translation, and supervises the translation program. A language textbook publisher employs assistant, associate, and senior editors as well as sales representatives, all of whom must have a knowledge of Spanish or French. One university press indicated a need for employees with skills in several different languages:

> Much of our business correspondence is in French, German, and Spanish. Contracts are often in French or German. It is sometimes useful to reply to foreign inquiries in the foreign language. We publish translations from several languages. . . . It would be helpful if our editors were fluent (as a staff) in French, German, Spanish, Italian, Czech, Russian, and Hebrew.

Even publishers who do not work regularly with foreign manuscripts or international publishing contracts recognize that their editors need foreign languages as part of their general training:

> Knowledge of a foreign language increases the value and potential contribution of a copy editor who works with manuscripts that contain foreign words or phrases or that can be improved by an occasional insertion of a foreign word or phrase.

A textbook publisher goes one step further: "We would seriously think twice about hiring someone who had taken no foreign language," he says, even though the company has only limited direct need for language skills. He considers proficiency in a second language as an indication of a broad education and the general ability of a prospective editorial employee. People who know a second language well are more likely to use their first language well, and facility with English is the skill most needed in publishing.

Several of the publishing firms surveyed by the MLA plan to expand their distribution efforts abroad; others anticipate an increase in the number of foreign books published here. One company expects that fluency in Russian will become more important in the publishing world and that new language demands will be made on the firm's staff. At least two publishers noted that they are already having trouble finding competent executives with foreign language skills. All of these respondents agreed that the right combination of editorial and foreign language skills may well mean good chances for employment in the publishing field in the 1980s.

Science

The English-speaking countries have no monopoly on scientific and technological progress. In fact, while English is still in the lead, Russian is now the second most important language of science. A survey of articles published in the physical, chemical, and biological sciences showed that 70 percent were written in English and about 20 percent in Russian, with the remaining 10 percent primarily in German and French.[11] It is true that many Russian

[11] I. L. Kosin, "The Growing Importance of Russian as a Language of Science," *BioScience* (American Institute of Biological Sciences), 22, No. 12 (December 1972), pp. 723-24.

scientific publications are abstracted in English, and a few journals are translated in their entirety. But any scientist making extensive use of research materials in chemistry, physics, geology, meteorology, mathematics, or the biological sciences—all areas in which Russian is the second most frequently used language—would, for many reasons, find it advantageous to learn Russian rather than to depend solely on translations for several reasons. First, the time lag between publication and translation averages a whole year, much too long for the scientist who must keep up with the latest developments in his field. In addition, the number of Russian scientific journals translated into English is very small compared to the total number published, and those that are translated and not simply abstracted are even fewer; relying only on translations means severely limiting one's resources. Finally, translations are expensive.

"Our [people] are busy now learning Russian, but we've found that conversational Russian and English are not going to be sufficient." Does this sound like a comment from a foreign study group? Actually, it was made by astronaut Charles Conrad, veteran of the Apollo and Skylab space exploration programs, while discussing the training program for a joint Soviet-American space venture. Astronauts and space technicians alike have found language to be one of the most serious obstacles in carrying out the project, and the scientific "language gap" may be even less thoroughly explored than outer space. Researchers might have to produce a Russian-American space-technical dictionary before training can be completed. But the space probe is only one of many examples of Russian-American collaboration in the sciences. As the two countries continue to replace political competition and hostility with cooperation and detente, they will most likely increase their joint research in such areas as medicine, sea and space exploration, and food and energy sources, thus eliminating wasteful duplication and combining talent and financial resources. The opportunities for international research teams may eventually be as diverse as the areas of science themselves, opening new doors for those scientists who are equipped with specialized language skills.

As America's industry becomes increasingly internationalized, so does its technology. Research chemists in a California pharmaceutical company cannot safely ignore discoveries in Germany, any more than they can those in New York. An engineering expert in an American branch of a Swiss company must understand and adapt designs sent from the home office. A mineral specialist for a Texas-based oil company may be called on to supervise a probe at an affiliate office in South America or to provide technical assistance to a counterpart in Saudi Arabia. To solve the problems of energy consumption and pollution, a physicist for a Detroit auto manufacturer may wish to consult with scientists and designers in Tokyo. The intermingling of international business and science is so extensive that even a brewery reports that it needs chemists, biochemists, and microbiologists, with skills in German, Italian, Spanish, and Japanese to work in its Minnesota plant. In short, the world of private industry is just one more source of employment for the scientist with training in a foreign language.

Service Occupations

Health Services

Doctors, nurses, laboratory technicians, medical assistants, and hospital administrators are finding more and more that a second language is important, and in some cases essential, in carrying out their duties.

Physicians may use foreign languages throughout medical school, research, internship, and clinical practice. American medical schools, limited in size and funds, have been unable to accommodate the growing number of potential medical students. As a result, many qualified students have had no choice but to study abroad. In 1977, some 6,200 Americans were working for their M.D. degrees at universities in Europe or Latin America, in such countries as Belgium, Italy, and Mexico. For most, the language barrier became a serious obstacle and a source of delay in their medical careers; for others, language skills acquired in school or college suddenly became a vital part of their professional progress.

Specialists in medical research need reading knowledge of languages in which research reports are written. Russian is now the second most frequently used language, after English, in research materials in the biological sciences, followed by German and French. While many articles in foreign languages are eventually translated into English by a centralized service, this is often a slow process, taking as long as twelve months, and in some highly specialized fields, a delay of this kind can seriously impede research.

In most large cities and in many rural areas internship and clinical practice increasingly bring doctors into contact with members of minority groups, new immigrants, and migrant workers who do not know English well enough to describe their symptoms or understand medical instructions. In recent years a number of hospitals all over the United States have arranged to hire bilingual personnel and to teach languages to doctors, nurses, administrators, and technicians. And where hospitals have been unable to do so for lack of incentive, funds, or personnel, staff members who speak only English have been feeling the "language gap" more and more.

For example, Georgetown University Hospital in Washington, D.C., now serves a large number of Spanish-speaking people. Jerome C. Ford of the Georgetown University School of Languages and Linguistics comments on the language problems encountered in the hospital:

> The need for foreign language speakers in the medical service area, especially of Spanish, is becoming more and more acute. The hospitals and clinics in the District of Columbia have already reached a point where Spanish-speaking personnel is not merely desirable but necessary. . . .
>
> We have a former Peace Corps volunteer at Georgetown Hospital whose service has proved invaluable. Unfortunately, she is but one individual and cannot work in all the wards at once. Word has gotten out that the hospital has a Spanish-speaking aide with the result that an increased number of non-English speakers have flocked to Georgetown rather than to the other hospitals in the area.[12]

One of the nurses at Georgetown replied, when asked if she had ever expected to need a foreign language while she was studying to be a nurse:

> Well, not really. I think you don't project yourself into a situation when you do interning. You tend

to . . . see yourself doing things and running a floor . . . and while a lot of your emphasis is on communication with the poor you don't see yourself actually talking.

Another of the Georgetown nurses stated:

> Most of the women coming to the clinic speak only Spanish. The language problem is huge. It really is. I know that's why I ended up originally taking some Spanish lessons.

Prospective health service workers, who may not have the time or opportunity to study languages while working, should anticipate early in their education a need for foreign language skills and, if possible, the language they will most likely be able to use.

The need for language skills is certainly not limited to Washington, D.C. A single Sunday edition of the *Los Angeles Times*, for instance, listed nine job openings for Spanish-speaking medical personnel: two medical assistants, two registered nurses, one medical receptionist, one optician, one dentist, one dental assistant, and one hospital housekeeping supervisor. In one Sunday edition of the *New York Times* there were eight positions advertised for medical workers with skills in Spanish, French, and Yiddish. These included two physicians, a hospital nutritionist, and a hospital admitting officer. And since health service skills are often in demand in developing countries, trainees with a basic knowledge of a foreign language and culture sometimes have the additional option of practicing their profession abroad. For example, Care, Inc., a service organization, has about fifty medical employees working overseas. Those placed in Latin America or in French-speaking countries must know Spanish or French before being assigned. Medical teams in such countries as Indonesia or Afghanistan are given intensive language instruction at the time of assignment.

Social Work

Social workers come into personal contact with people who need help with problems such as poverty, unemployment, child abuse, poor housing, or illness. Most social service agencies, both public and private, are in cities where

---

[12] Jerome C. Ford, letter to the authors, 9 May 1973.

there are concentrations of minority groups and immigrants, and many employ social workers who speak a second language. To work with a Puerto Rican family in New York City or in a Mexican-American neighborhood in California, for instance, a social worker cannot possibly win trust—or sometimes even begin a case—without knowing Spanish. In most cities, social workers without a second language are limited in the kinds of work they can do, and in some cases they are also limited in their chances of being hired. For example, the New York Association for New Americans, Inc., a private agency that helps immigrants deal with their new environment, requires caseworkers, vocational counselors, and supervisors who speak the languages of their clients. Cancer Care, which helps the families of cancer patients, recommends that social workers in the New York City area know Spanish and Italian. Travelers Aid International Social Service of America has an international casework service, requiring staff with reading and writing skills in several languages and with conversational ability in Chinese and Spanish for interviewing clients at its home office in New York. State and local government service agencies, schools, hospitals, rehabilitation centers, and community action programs all may need bilingual or multilingual personnel, depending on the language groups present in the community.

Religious Occupations

The American Association of Theological Schools recommends that people planning to become Protestant ministers focus their college studies on the liberal arts, *including* foreign languages. Those who wish to become Catholic priests must take two years of high school Latin, and the study of a modern language is encouraged. Jewish seminaries require Hebrew, and in many cases students make use of scholarly works written in French or German.

In missionary work, knowledge of a foreign language is crucial to those who also have the necessary religious training—and often experience in various social service fields—in order to carry out their work in countries around the world, particularly in Africa and Asia. The executive secretary of a mission association which has more than fifty member organizations has stated:

All of these organizations which send missionaries abroad find it imperative that the majority of their workers learn one, two, or three languages in order to minister effectively in the country to which they are sent.

Because much missionary work is done in countries whose languages are rarely taught in the United States or where the language is complicated by many different dialects, missionaries are sometimes not required to learn a language until they are assigned to a particular area. For example, although the entire staff of the Overseas Missionary Fellowship, except for a few members "on the homeside," know at least one foreign language, their actual language learning is done in the countries in which they work. In such cases, studying even the "wrong" language in school would familiarize the future missionary with the *way* languages are learned, an invaluable preparation for a career during which several different languages may be needed. And in twenty-two African countries French, as the former colonial language, is still the primary vehicle for establishing initial contacts with national and local government.

Other Service Organizations

Many different types of service organizations need people with language skills for work both in the United States and abroad. Again, language skills must accompany other skills—usually in the fields of social work, health care, or administration. The American Friends Service Committee, the service agency of the Religious Society of Friends (Quakers), has centers in several countries that conduct institutes and seminars on world peace, arrange social welfare programs, and sponsor projects of technical assistance in such areas as housing, medicine, and agriculture. A worker must first be qualified in a particular profession—for example, as a teacher or medical assistant. In addition, notes the Director for Overseas Placement, many positions also require a foreign language:

Of the 65 expatriate staff we have appointed abroad, roughly one-third require fluency in the language of the area to which they are assigned. . . . Our recruitment efforts are geared to finding staff already in possession of a needed foreign language skill, supplemented by field office arrangements for local tutorial or short course training as needed.

A Catholic service agency also employs people who need a second language as an adjunct skill for work abroad:

> Foreign language skills are very necessary to the jobs being done by [our] representatives . . . overseas since they have continual contact with local government, intergovernmental, United Nations, and other international bodies at work in their countries of assignment. In many areas, it is impossible for these people to function effectively in English. We place a steady and constant emphasis on foreign language skills in the persons we hire as career staff. At present it seems difficult to find the right combination of language and administrative skills.

At home, there are also areas where service organizations employ people with foreign language skills. The Lutheran Council in the U.S.A., for instance, has a Department of Latin American Publication for the dissemination of literature abroad and a Department of Immigration and Refugee Service to provide help for new arrivals in the United States; in both, "the foreign languages used are vitally important." Organizations such as the YWCA, YMCA, Salvation Army, and Red Cross on occasion need speakers of foreign languages, although experience in particular jobs is, again, given higher priority.

Social Sciences

Anthropologists are involved in the study of people, their origins, cultures, traditions, languages, beliefs, values, and social relationships. They frequently combine research and field work with teaching in colleges and universities, but some anthropologists work for museums, private industry, and federal and state agencies. Most hold a graduate degree, preferably a doctorate. Researchers specializing in cultural anthropology often live with remote or unusual groups of people—for example, a nomadic group in Africa, an Indian tribe in South America, or a nation of island dwellers in the South Pacific—to learn their ways of life and to understand the patterns of human culture, the contrasts between societies, and the stages of development of modern society. To achieve any depth of understanding, it is essential that cultural anthropologists be fluent in the language of the people they are studying. Other anthropologists are archaeologists, who study past societies through the physical remnants they left behind such as tools, buildings, furniture, and art. The research of archaeologists take them all over the world, and to excavate a Mayan city in Mexico, for example, or prehistoric relics in Asia Minor, an archaeologist should know the language of the area. Finally, some anthropologists specialize in linguistics, the science of language structure and the historical relationships among languages. Obviously, knowledge of several languages is basic to this work.

Political scientists study government at all levels, from local and county to national and international. Foreign language skills are important primarily to those who are concerned with international relations and foreign political systems. They may be teachers, researchers for private and government organizations, foreign service officers for the federal government, or, in a few instances, advisors to government officials. In whatever capacity, political scientists need a close acquaintance with the history, culture, and language of one or more foreign countries. When such knowledge is lacking, a political specialist may be restricted to interpreting world events through the American perspective only, ignoring the cultural differences that give rise to political differences.

Marshall Shulman, formerly Director of the Russian Institute at Columbia University and now serving with the Department of State, feels that this sort of narrow view was responsible for some major difficulties encountered during the Vietnam War:

> . . . one reason we were not in a position to make sensible judgments about the issue as it arose in the middle 1960s is that in the entire country we did not have a handful of people who knew the language, the policies or the culture of Vietnam. Our decisions were made in ignorance.

He fears that similar problems are likely to arise in our dealings with Russia unless more political experts are trained in the Russian language and culture. And this concern can be extended to American relations with China,

Japan, the Arab nations, and, indeed, any other foreign country. To develop intelligent attitudes and policies, there must be political scientists and government advisors who are familiar with all areas of these countries' cultures, including their languages.

Sociologists study the organization and behavior of groups in human society. In their dealings with two groups in particular—immigrants and minorities—the ability to speak a foreign language is a great advantage. A sociologist who speaks Polish, for example, brings to a case study on Polish immigrants the ability to gather data firsthand in the Polish community and to determine, based on conversations and contacts, what linguistic and cultural differences are likely to benefit or hinder Polish immigrants in the United States. Similarly, a sociologist doing research on the organization of family life among Chinese-Americans would be at a disadvantage without a speaking knowledge of Chinese. But research is only one area where a sociologist may need language skills; they may also open the door to a number of public service jobs, as indicated in this report from a professor of social science in Los Angeles:

> Almost every sociology major of Spanish-speaking background who has graduated from our school in the last six years and gone on to finish the bachelor's degree is now employed in some type of work with people of Spanish language background. The Social Security Administration is also asking our school for young people who can serve as interpreters, as are also the Public Defender's Office, the night courts and the Immigration and Naturalization Bureau.

Travel and Tourism

Industries connected with travel and tourism are increasingly feeling the need for employees who speak foreign languages. In 1978, over 19.8 million people from abroad visited this country, an increase of 560 percent over the 3 million foreign visitors traveling to the United States in 1972. With the devaluation of the dollar and increased prosperity in most European countries and Japan, as well as the mushrooming of an assortment of package tours that provide air travel, hotel accommodations, and sightseeing excursions at extremely low prices, travel to the United States has become possible for even more people from around the world. The *New York Times* first noted signs of this unexpected "invasion" in 1973:

> The summer of 1973 may well be remembered in the tourist circles as the summer of the flip-flop, when the mass movement of Americans flocking abroad for vacations reversed itself and a new immigration of European and other foreign businessmen came flooding into New York.

The celebration of the American Bicentennial in 1976 attracted even more foreign tourists; yet the American travel industry and the American population as a whole, were—and are still—largely unprepared in terms of language competence for this influx of foreign visitors. International travel agents indicated in a survey that language is one of the most serious problems in selling travel in the United States to foreign residents. In Latin America, it was the foremost problem. In Mexico, reports a U.S. government official, "sixty percent of all potential visitors to the United States expect language to be a barrier and therefore hesitate to undertake this travel."

The language barrier is not only a problem in attracting tourists; it is also a problem in keeping them happy while they are here. Countless inconveniences plague foreign visitors when no one speaks their language, and their opportunities to become acquainted with the American people are greatly reduced when they are restricted to guided tours and communication with members of the tour group. An item on foreign visitors in the *New York Times* (18 March 1973) elaborates on these problems:

> Many foreigners here suffer more than a little inconvenience, a great deal of it due to language problems. Most Americans cannot say even the most rudimentary guidebook phrases in any language save their own. Even more serious is the failure of the so-called hospitality industries to provide adequate bilingual, not to mention multilingual, personnel and services. And the language difficulties serve to exacerbate ordinary day-to-day problems: what otherwise could easily be overlooked becomes annoying and frustrating.

But efforts *are* being made to overcome the language barrier by placing bilingual and multilingual personnel in various travel industries and by creating new services that require employees with language skills. For example, a Multilingual Port Receptionist Program, sponsored by the U.S. Travel Service in conjunction with several local agencies, employs multilingual students as receptionists at major airports in Seattle, San Juan, and New York. They help incoming foreign visitors go through customs and immigration procedures and make travel connections. Their salaries are paid partly by the U.S. Travel Service and partly out of funds from the Office of Education's college work-study program. Another new service is Travel Phone USA, which provides a nationwide toll-free telephone interpreter service in Spanish, French, German, and Japanese. This too is sponsored by the U.S. Travel Service, in conjunction with Travelodge International and Pan American Airways, and is currently assisting guests from abroad as well as airlines, hotels, and police. An expansion of such services can be anticipated. As the hotel, motel, tourism, and transportation industries equip themselves for the new surge of foreign visitors (estimated to reach nearly 23 million annually within the next few years), they will undoubtedly expect to give employment preference to persons with foreign language skills.

Hotels and Motels

A front desk clerk who registers a new guest, a manager who must deal with a client's complaint, a telephone operator placing an overseas call, an information clerk giving directions to the nearest tourist attraction—these are just a few examples of situations in which language skills are vital in dealing with guests from abroad. Hotel administrators, clerks, switchboard operators, and restaurant personnel can greatly improve their services to foreign visitors—and their establishment's reputation—by knowing a foreign language. This fact has been recognized by the United States Travel Service, a division of the Department of Commerce, which in 1977 requested the publisher of one of the most popular U.S. travel guide series to include information on language capabilities of staff in the hotels and motels it evaluates. As a result, the *Mobil Travel Guides* now routinely identify establishments which can handle visitors speaking German, French, Italian, Spanish, and Japanese.

One hotel that became aware early of the need for bilingual staff members is the Statler Hilton Hotel in New York City. Its director of agency and tour sales explained the hotel's policies to the *New York Times*:

> I think one of the major criteria in hiring people for the hotel is their knowledge of languages. . . . We now have employees here who speak 36 languages and that isn't an accident. The reception desk has a list of staff, what languages they speak and when and where they work. If we need their help we can get them in seconds. Too often in the past foreigners have been treated as second-class citizens. I know how that feels and I think we've had enough of it.[13]

The General Manager of the Conrad Hilton Hotel in Chicago notes that while language ability is not a requirement for all hotel jobs, it is almost always an advantage:

> I can think of no other industry where the ability to converse in a foreign language would be more applicable than in the hotel industry. The Conrad Hilton has long recognized the value of having a sufficient number of personnel on its staff who do carry with them this particular talent in an employment situation. We, of course, receive guests from virtually every nation, and . . . we have found our overall language capabilities to be of great assistance as well as being highly appreciated by our international guests.

His establishment has some employees who are fluent in as many as five different languages, and multilingual personnel are placed in such guest-contact positions as room clerk, lobby manager, front office clerk, and banquet managers. If guests need personal help, the name of an employee who speaks that guest's language can be found on a special list of staff members who have language skills. Over twenty languages are on that list, from the more common languages to Romanian, Czech, Chinese, Russian, Swedish, Dutch, Ilocano, and Tagalog.

Transportation

The ever growing American tourist trade would not be possible, of course, without the international airlines, which schedule hundreds of flights to and from the United States each week (more than 600 on the North Atlantic

[13] *New York Times*, 25 March 1973.

25

route alone). The most obvious use of foreign languages is among the flight attendants for most international airlines. Not only are the standard pre-departure and in-flight announcements made in at least two languages for most intercontinental flights, but the growing number of foreign tourists on both the overseas and domestic flights of U.S. airlines require flight attendants with language ability for dealing with passengers in in-flight situations. Ground hosts and hostesses, flight announcers, information and reservations clerks, and other international airport personnel who come into contact with foreign tourists are, in some cases, required to speak a foreign language; in many other cases, language skills are recommended or preferred. Telephone information personnel, too, may frequently need language skills when assisting travelers who do not speak English. And employees of several domestic airlines need Spanish for both ground and in-flight work, particularly in connection with flights to and from Puerto Rico and Florida.

Other transportation industries have varying needs for language skills. Train and bus lines, for example, sometimes need bilingual information, reservation, and ticket personnel in areas where there are large minority groups. Ship lines have some need for bilingual personnel in dealing with foreign passengers. And language skills may soon play an important role in an auxiliary transportation industry, that of guided tours, already an institution in virtually every European country and beginning to develop here with the influx of foreign tourists to America.

LANGUAGE AS PRIMARY SKILL

Foreign Language Teaching

Approximately 80,000 Americans earn at least part of their living by teaching foreign languages and literature; approximately 50,000 teach in junior and senior high schools, 25,000 in colleges and universities, several thousand in elementary schools, and the remainder in commercial and government-operated language schools. The greatest number teach Spanish, followed in order by French, German, Latin, Russian, Italian, Chinese, Greek, and Japanese. In addition, a sizeable number teach English to Americans who speak languages other than English as their native tongue—more than 22.5 million Chicanos, Eskimos, Puerto Ricans, Navajos, and others (according to the 1970 census). Still others teach in bilingual education programs, in which students follow a regular academic program in both their native language and in English; most frequently, these are elementary or junior high school programs.

For a variety of reasons, the job market for foreign language teachers, except in the fields of Asian languages, bilingual education, and TESOL (teaching of English to speakers of other languages), has become restricted and competitive. Frequently school districts now require prospective foreign language teachers to have at least a bachelor's degree with a major in one or two foreign languages or with a major in one language and a major or minor in another field that they can also teach, (mathematics, for instance), plus appropriate education courses, some experience in practice teaching, a teaching certificate from the state, and prior travel or residence in the foreign country. Usually teachers of foreign languages in elementary school (FLES), unlike most other elementary school teachers, are subject specialists; they teach only foreign languages. However, they are required to have professional training for elementary school teaching; only a small number of colleges in the country offer such training.

At present, teachers just out of college may have an easier time finding jobs than many of their more experienced colleagues; not only are they more willing to move to where jobs are available (rural areas, smaller suburbs, inner city areas), but their starting salaries are also much lower—an asset from the school district's point of view. Private and parochial schools frequently hire noncertified teachers and may provide smaller classes and sometimes better working conditions, but their pay scales are generally lower than public schools' while their other requirements may be just as stringent. The national median salary for secondary school teachers in 1976-77 was $13,230, but in large districts salaries for teachers with a great deal of experience and some administrative duties can be as high as $25-30,000 a year.

The field of Asian languages, because of recent interest in non-Western cultures, has been expanding since the early 1960s; however, these languages still account for fewer than ten percent of all college students enrolled in foreign languages and even fewer at the high school level. The fields of bilingual education and TESOL have expanded dramatically since the federal government, through the Bilingual Education Act of 1967, to finance educational programs designed specifically for children of limited English-speaking ability. By 1978, the U.S. Office of Bilingual Education was supporting projects in 565 school districts across the nation, had funded 42 Bilingual Centers providing support services, and offered financial and other assistance to various bilingual programs organized by state departments of education in all fifty states plus Puerto Rico, the Trust Territories, American Samoa, and Guam. Several states, notably Pennsylvania, Louisiana, and Massachusetts, have also passed bilingual education legislation in recent years — some of it even more comprehensive than the federal legislation.

Teachers in bilingual education programs must be fluent in both languages, sensitive to both cultures, and qualified to teach as elementary school teachers or in a specific subject area: frequently noncertified persons with native fluency are hired as teacher aides. TESOL teachers must undergo a specific training program that includes comparative linguistics if they are to be certified to teach in public schools. Recently some organizations such as local YMCA's and chambers of commerce have started TESOL programs, and a number of commercial language schools specialize in teaching English to speakers of other languages. Since there are sometimes local shortages of qualified bilingual or TESOL teachers, school districts may grant one-year emergency certification and allow the teacher to earn regular certification while teaching.

In the past few years, job opportunities at the four-year college level have become increasingly scarce. Professors at four-year colleges are usually expected to have completed or to be completing doctoral programs, including the dissertation, and they must continue scholarly research and publication throughout their careers. Salaries range from $11,000 to over $26,000, with the national median salary for nine months of teaching falling at $18,462 in 1977-78. Graduate students, especially at large universities, often can support themselves and gain experience by teaching undergraduate language courses. Occasionally colleges will hire people who have completed only the bachelor's degree to teach courses — in Romanian, for example — for which there are few qualified teachers and little student demand. These positions are usually part-time, preference is often given to natives, and the pay is usually low.

Professors at the rapidly growing number of two-year colleges are required by some states to have teaching certificates; almost invariably they are also required to have completed master's degree programs and sometimes doctoral programs. Requirements for research and publication are less stringent than at the four-year colleges, and teaching loads are consequently much heavier. Salaries are generally somewhat lower than at four-year colleges.

Commercial and government-operated language schools generally prefer to hire native speakers as teachers, and most positions, at least in the commercial language schools, are part-time. There are over thirty commercial language schools in New York City alone, several of them very large.

Interpreting and Translating

Interpreters and translators are employed everywhere in the world — by the United States and other governments, the United Nations, international conferences, trade councils, publishers, and many other businesses and organizations. Translators deal with written material and interpreters with oral communication. Foreign languages are obviously essential tools of the translating and interpreting professions, but knowing a foreign language, even extremely well, is no guarantee that one will be a good translator. Professional translators and interpreters need an exceptionally fluent command of English and at least one, and more frequently two, foreign languages; a working knowledge of the subject matter of their material (chemistry, international law, or automobile manufacturing, for example); familiarity with the cultures represented; a good writing style or pleasing voice; and frequently a great deal of creativity, especially if translating poetry or fiction. Special training is generally required, and programs leading to diplomas or certificates in translating and interpreting are available at a number of American colleges and universities, among them Georgetown, Stanford, Stephens College (Missouri), and the Monterey (California) Institute of Foreign Studies. Brown University, Carnegie-Mellon University, Rutgers University (Camden branch), Marygrove College (Michigan), and Notre Dame College of Ohio also offer courses in translating. In Canada, Laval University, the University of Montreal, McGill University, and Laurentian University grant diplomas in translation, and degree programs in Europe are offered by the Ecole d'Interprètes Internationaux in Mons, Belgium; by the Ecole Supérieure d'Interprètes et de Traducteurs at the University of Paris; by the Dolmetscherinstitut at the University of Heidelberg in Germany; and by the University of Geneva's Ecole de Traduction et d'Interprétation in Switzerland.

Translators and interpreters are employed in various agencies of the United States Government. By far the largest staff of language specialists in the federal government is in the Language Services Division of the Department of State. Here a sizeable number of qualified linguists serve as interpreters and translators at official talks and conferences and during escort assignments, using both the simultaneous and consecutive systems of translation. Interpreters are required to be especially fluent and have no obvious accent. Translators into English usually must have a fluent knowledge of at least two foreign languages; translators into foreign languages are required to translate from English into only one other language, but they must be able to write in that language with exceptional skill. Escort interpreters may be called upon to accompany foreign leaders and technicians on their travels within the United States and to interpret for them at their professional interviews and meetings; these jobs are usually temporary, lasting from three days to three months.

The Federal Bureau of Investigation and the Immigration and Naturalization Service both employ full-time interpreters and the FBI employs some translators. An unspecified number of language specialists work at the Central Intelligence Agency. Other departments in the United States government use either the Language Services Division of the Department of State or staff members who happen to be bilingual to meet their language needs—in translating correspondence, legislation, or court proceedings, for example.

The United Nations maintains a large staff of interpreters and translators, hired by competitive examination. Interpreters must have a thorough knowledge of three of the United Nations' six official languages: Arabic, Chinese, English, French, Russian, and Spanish. Most often they interpret from a foreign language into their native language in both the consecutive and simultaneous systems. Both translators and interpreters must have a college degree, experience in their work, and a broad knowledge of general culture, politics, economics, and law.

Some businesses that have extensive international connections maintain a small translating staff, or employ one full-time translator, to work in such areas as marketing or publication. And a growing number of professional translation agencies serve businesses and individuals who may occasionally need translation services. Generally this work is technical in nature and requires technical knowledge on the part of the translator. Translators for privately owned agencies may sometimes be part of a full-time staff or, more frequently, work on a part-time or free-lance basis. Translators who have acquired a reputation for their skill may be awarded a contract to translate fiction or poetry; this type of work requires considerable creative and linguistic talent, and opportunities in this field are quite rare.

SUMMARY

With the growing involvement of the United States in international business and the increasingly multinational character of American society itself, the importance of foreign languages in nearly every kind of occupation is evident. The New York City bus driver who deals daily with both city residents and foreign tourists who speak a variety of languages, the automobile executive marketing products abroad, the scientist using foreign research material, the social worker assigned to a Spanish-speaking neighborhood, the draftsman converting a European design to American measurements, the flight attendant on a trans-Atlantic run, the foreign service officer in Asia, the restaurant manager greeting a group of Japanese visitors, the publisher drawing up a contract with an Italian novelist, the television producer of Spanish-language specials—the number of Americans who use a foreign language in their work is virtually unlimited.

Generally, American business firms and service organizations are not likely to hire employees on the basis of language skills alone. But a substantial number of them have come to recognize their specific needs for foreign languages, and most of them foresee a growth in the need for language skills, both in their own particular businesses and in the general employment market. And if there is one thing that employers can agree on in regard to the future, it is change—change in the size, scope, and direction of their businesses and change in the talents they will demand. Success in the world of work may very well depend on the ability of an employee to adapt to changing requirements—to convert general training and potential abilities into active, productive skills. Engineers whose knowledge of German comes in handy every so often this year may find in five years that their language skills are as valuable to their companies as their technical abilities. And junior administrators for city hospitals may find themselves obliged to look for new jobs when Spanish becomes a requirement for their positions—and they don't have it.

More and more students and teachers have begun to recognize the value of school and college experience as preparation for work—for a trade, occupation, or profession. This preparation should include learning about work, learning basic skills necessary for work, and eventually learning specific skills for a specific kind of work. The more varied and highly developed one's skills are, the broader one's options become. Knowledge of a foreign language, a traditional part of the liberal arts education, is at the same time an important part of the basic preparation for a wide variety of careers. The student who misses an opportunity to learn a foreign language is, in short, closing doors and narrowing career opportunities.

For many people, the ideal time to begin learning a second language is in elementary school, but the traditional high school sequence can also be effective and profitable, especially if the student understands the value of language study for both general developments and career orientation. Many high schools are, in fact, beginning to relate language study directly to the world of work, offering such courses as Commercial Spanish, Secretarial French, or Scientific German. One high school located near an international airport integrates aviation- and aerospace-related vocabulary into all of its language courses as a matter of routine and invites bilingual flight attendants to help out in the language resource center. A high school in the Southwest offers a number of foreign language vocational courses, including Spanish for Ranch and Farm Workers, Spanish for Education, Interpreting and Translating, Medical Terminology in Spanish, French in the World of Fashion, Foreign Language for Music Majors, Bilingual Secretarial Training, and Spanish Vocabulary for the Construction and Building Trades. A junior high school in the East has incorporated a study of local vocational needs as well as a job-related vocabulary into its eighth grade French program. And career-related foreign language mini-courses are steadily on the rise in high schools across the country, providing a "taste" of a number of career possibilities for the language student.

The college language course may also provide effective career preparation, especially since college students have usually begun to narrow down their occupational choices and can relate foreign language study to specific career needs. Many two-year colleges and universities have introduced career-related courses into their language curricula, some of which count toward a major in foreign languages. In other cases a double major or a minor in foreign languages can be useful. A major in journalism, sociology, business administration, or medicine combined with a minor in Spanish or Russian, for example, would be good preparation for many of the jobs described in this report. A language major, too, can be useful for a nonlanguage career. Law, medical, and business schools, for example, are happy to accept people with undergraduate majors in any of the liberal arts, including foreign languages. And employers from almost every area of the business world indicate that they would consider a language major as a suitable — and sometimes preferable — background for employees or trainees, provided the candidates have also demonstrated aptitude for the more technical aspects of the work they would be expected to do. The following testimonial from a graduate with a language major from a midwestern university helps to illustrate this point:

> To demonstrate the importance of linguistic proficiency to multinational corporations, let me relate to you briefly the circumstances surrounding my obtaining a position with _____ Rubber Company. When my wife and I decided . . . that we would like to live in _____ I called the local Chamber of Commerce and inquired as to which companies there had extensive multinational operations. I was told that both _____ and _____ had substantial subsidiary operations abroad. I then called _____ and spoke to the marketing manager in the International Division, explaining my qualifications, and, in fact, asked if a position was available. I explained that I was fluent in both Spanish and Portuguese and had some practical business experience. . . . My linguistic ability in Spanish was tested immediately. A Cuban woman was asked to examine me over the telephone for proficiency. Having passed this preliminary examination, I was allowed to submit my application for employment along with my resume.
>
> Within a few days I was invited to an interview. When I arrived, I was told from the onset that no decision would be made during my visit, since other applicants with a far greater technical knowledge had yet to be interviewed. Nevertheless, after a few minutes speaking with the head of the International Marketing Staff, I was allowed to speak with the Vice President for Latin American Operations. This interview was conducted in Portuguese. Within five minutes after the conclusion of this interview, I was presented to the Vice President for European Operations. This interview was conducted in both English and Spanish and I am sure my having lived abroad in Mexico . . . was an additional plus in my favor. Fifteen minutes later I was offered the position.
>
> As it was explained to me, although there were many applicants more qualified than I in terms of technical expertise in the rubber industry, it had been _____'s experience after many years of not-so-successful attempts in training their personnel in languages, that it would be easier to train me in the technical end of the rubber business, than to train an expert to speak Spanish and Portuguese.
>
> I am sure that my experience in obtaining a job is not unique or isolated. Today, industry and commerce are becoming extremely multinational. Of the top five hundred corporations in the United States, an estimated 80 percent have subsidiaries or financial interests abroad. . . . From my own knowledge, I could list thirty large concerns with active multinational interests and divisions. Caterpillar, General Motors, United States Steel, Kraftco, General Foods, Kodak, just to name a few, all have large international operations.

Whether a college major or minor, a four-year high school sequence, or a preparation beginning as far back as primary school, an education in foreign languages is not just an exercise in grammar and literature, nor does it provide the background for just a few very specialized jobs. It is actually a vital preparation for a growing number of careers.

Other less tangible values of language study are well known to students, teachers, and others who enjoy words and appreciate the special insights that the study of words, word origins, and linguistics gives them. Language study is pleasurable and valuable in itself because it furnishes the key to the thinking patterns, culture, and social institutions of a foreign nation or nations; because it affords insights into the nature of language itself, and into the human mind as well; because it fosters a sense of shared humanity among persons who have learned to break down the barriers that impede communication. In addition, language expands and enhances the pleasures of travel, of good literature and the arts, and of social interaction. By combining career aspirations with the humanizing and broadening effects of the study of foreign language and culture, one can make a sound investment in a stimulating and rewarding future.

MATERIALS RELATING TO
CAREERS USING LANGUAGES

Most of the publications listed below are up-dated frequently. Except for the *Occupational Outlook Handbook*, most of the materials available through the U.S. Government Printing Office range in price from 50¢ to $1.50; interested persons should write directly to the Government Printing Office or visit one of the GPO Bookstores (located in twenty major cities) for a recent price list and for information on new materials published since this list was prepared.

American Students and Teachers Abroad: Sources of Information about Overseas Study, Teaching, Work, and Travel. Washington, D.C.: Government Printing Office.

A Career in the Foreign Service. Washington, D.C.: Government Printing Office.

Careers in Foreign Languages: A Handbook By June L. Sherif. New York: Regents Publishing Co., 1975. Available in paperback.

Careers in the U.S. Foreign Service. Chicago: Institute for Research, 1976.

Directory of American Firms Operating in Foreign Countries. Edited by Juvenal L. Angel. New York: World Trade Academy Press, 1975.

Directory of Foreign Firms Operating in the United States. Edited by Juvenal L. Angel. New York: World Trade Academy Press, 1971.

Directory of International Agencies. Edited by Juvenal L. Angel. New York: World Trade Academy Press, 1971.

Foreign Languages and Your Career. By Edward Bourgoin. Washington, D.C.: Columbia Language Services, 1978.

"Foreign Language Majors: The Washington Perspective." By Allen L. Weinstein. In *ADFL Bulletin*, Vol. 6, No. 4 (May 1975), pp. 18-27.

Guide to Foreign Medical Schools. New York: Institute of International Education.

International Educational and Cultural Exchange. Washington, D.C.: Government Printing Office. Issued annually.

International Medical Programs Available to American Medical Students. Chantilly, Va.: American Medical Students Association. (P.O. Box 131, 14650 Lee Rd., Chantilly, Va. 22021.)

Interpretation Please. By Mary De Lavergne. Washington, D.C.: Government Printing Office.

Interpreters and Translators. Moravia, N.Y.: Chronicle Guidance Publications, 1977.

"Language-Oriented Careers in the Federal Government." By Carol S. Fuller. In *ADFL Bulletin*, Vol. 6, No. 1 (Sept. 1974), pp. 45-51.

Languages for the World of Work: An Annotated Bibliography. By M. Rex Arnett. Salt Lake City, Utah: Olympus Research Corp., 1975.

Looking for Employment in Foreign Countries. By Juvenal L. Angel. New York: World Trade Academy Press, 1972.

Overseas Employment Opportunities for Educators. Alexandria, Va.: Overseas Dependents Schools, U.S. Department of Defense.

Occupational Briefs: Earning a Living with Foreign Languages. Moravia, N.Y.: Chronicle Guidance Publications, 1977.

Occupational Outlook Handbook. Washington, D.C.: Government Printing Office.

Opportunities in Foreign Language Careers. By Theodore Heubner. Louisville, Ky.: Vocational Guidance Manuals, 1975.

The Professional Diplomat. By J. E. Harr. Princeton, N.J.: Princeton Univ. Press, 1969.

Student Travel Catalog. New York: Council on International Educational Exchange.

Teaching Abroad. New York: Institute of International Education.

"Translation as a Career Option for Foreign Language Majors." By Royal L. Tinsley, Jr. In *ADFL Bulletin*, Vol. 7, No. 4 (May 1976), pp. 25-33.

Whole World Handbook: A Student Guide to Work, Study, and Travel Abroad. New York: Council on International Educational Exchange.

USEFUL ADDRESSES

American Graduate School of International Management, Glendale, Ariz. 85306

ACTION (Peace Corps and VISTA Programs), Personnel Management Division, Washington, D.C. 20525

Agency for International Development, Office of Personnel and Manpower, Washington, D.C. 20037

American Council on the Teaching of Foreign Languages (ACTFL), 2 Park Avenue, Suite 1814, New York, N.Y. 10016.

American Translators Association, P.O. Box 129, Croton-on-Hudson, N.Y. 10520

Association of Departments of Foreign Languages (ADFL), 62 Fifth Avenue, New York, N.Y. 10011

Committee on International Relations, National Education Association, 1201 Sixteenth Street, N.W., Washington, D.C. 20036

Council on International Educational Exchange, 777 United Nations Plaza, New York, N.Y. 10017

Defense Language Institute, Civilian Personnel Office, Fort Sam Houston, Texas 78234

International Communication Agency, Recruitment and Source Development Division, 1776 Pennsylvania Avenue, N.W., Washington, D.C. 20547

Institute of International Education, 809 United Nations Plaza, New York, N.Y. 10017

Institute of International Studies, U.S. Office of Education, Department of Health, Education, and Welfare, Washington, D.C. 20201

Latin American Institute, 292 Madison Avenue, New York, N.Y. 10017

Overseas Dependents Schools, Department of Defense, 2461 Eisenhower Avenue, Alexandria, Va. 22331

Teachers of English to Speakers of Other La (TESOL), School of Languages and Lin Georgetown University, Washington, D.C

United Nations, Office of Personnel, Nev N.Y. 10017

U.S. Civil Service Commission, Washingto 20415

U.S. Department of State, Foreign Service ment Division, Washington, D.C. 20520

U.S. Government Printing Office, Washingto 20402